Sales Mastery:

Techniques for Building and Sustaining a High-Performing Sales Team"

By Saba Isah

Introduction

Sales is one of the most important functions of any business. Whether you are selling products or services, your ability to master the art of selling can have a direct impact on your success as a business owner, entrepreneur or sales professional. In this book, we will explore the essential elements of sales mastery and provide practical tips and strategies to help you achieve your sales goals.

Table of contents

Chapter 1; The psychology of sales mastery

❖ Understanding the psychology of selling

The psychology of selling is the study of why people buy, what motivates them to make purchasing decisions, and how salespeople can use this understanding to influence those decisions. Here are some key psychological principles that can be useful for salespeople:

- Establishing rapport: People are more likely to buy from someone they like and trust. Building a positive relationship with the prospect through active listening, empathy, and genuine interest in their needs and concerns can help establish trust and rapport.

- Understanding the prospect's needs: Effective salespeople take the time to understand the prospect's needs, wants, and pain points. By doing so, they can present their product or service as a solution to the prospect's problem.

- Highlighting benefits over features: People are more interested in the benefits of a product or service rather than its features. For example, instead of focusing on the technical specifications of a computer, a salesperson could highlight how the computer will improve the prospect's productivity or entertainment experience.

- Using social proof: People are often influenced by the actions of others. By highlighting positive reviews, testimonials, or case studies, salespeople can provide social proof that their product or service has worked for others.

- Addressing objections: Prospects may have concerns or objections about the product or service. Effective salespeople listen to these concerns and address them by providing information or solutions that alleviate the prospect's fears or doubts.
- Creating a sense of urgency: People are more likely to act when they feel a sense of urgency or scarcity. Salespeople can create this sense of urgency by highlighting limited-time offers, scarcity of supply, or the consequences of delaying a purchasing decision.

- Using emotional appeals: People often make purchasing decisions based on emotional factors rather than rational ones. Effective salespeople appeal to the prospect's emotions by highlighting how the product or service can make them feel, such as happy, secure, or confident.

❖ Developing a sales mindset

Developing a sales mindset is about adopting a positive attitude and a set of behaviors that are focused on achieving sales success. Here are some key steps to develop a sales mindset:

- Set clear goals: Successful salespeople set clear goals that are specific, measurable, achievable, relevant, and time-bound (SMART). By setting clear goals, salespeople can focus their efforts and track their progress towards achieving those goals.

- Cultivate a positive attitude: A positive attitude is essential for success in sales. Salespeople should focus on their strengths, stay motivated, and maintain a growth mindset that is open to learning and development.

- Develop a deep understanding of the product or service: Successful salespeople have a deep understanding of the product or service they are selling. They know the features, benefits, and limitations of the product or service and can articulate how it can solve the customer's problem.

- Build relationships: Sales is not just about selling a product or service; it is about building relationships. Successful salespeople build trust and rapport with their customers by understanding their needs, concerns, and goals.

- Focus on providing value: Successful salespeople focus on providing value to their customers rather than just making a sale. They take a consultative approach, listening to their customers' needs, and providing tailored solutions that meet those needs.

- Embrace rejection: Rejection is a part of sales, and successful salespeople learn to embrace it. They use rejection as an opportunity to learn, improve, and refine their approach.

- Continuously learn and improve: Successful salespeople are always learning and improving. They seek out new knowledge, skills, and techniques to enhance their sales abilities and stay ahead of the competition.

By adopting these behaviors and attitudes, salespeople can develop a sales mindset that is focused on achieving success through building relationships, providing value, and continuous learning and improvement.

By understanding these psychological principles, salespeople can build trust, address concerns, and create a sense of urgency that can influence the prospect's purchasing decision.

❖ Overcoming limiting beliefs and fear

Limiting beliefs and fear can hold salespeople back from achieving their full potential. Here are some strategies to overcome these barriers:

- Identify and challenge limiting beliefs: The first step in overcoming limiting beliefs is to identify them. Limiting beliefs are often subconscious and can be difficult to recognize. Salespeople should ask themselves what beliefs they hold about themselves, their product or service, or their industry that may be limiting their success. Once identified, they should challenge those beliefs by asking themselves whether they are true, and whether they are helping or hindering their sales success.

- Reframe negative self-talk: Negative self-talk is a common barrier to success in sales. Salespeople should learn to recognize when they are engaging in negative self-talk and reframe those thoughts in a more positive and constructive way. For example, instead of thinking "I'm not good at sales," they could reframe it as "I'm still learning and improving my sales skills."

- Practice visualization and positive affirmations: Visualization and positive affirmations can help salespeople overcome fear and build confidence. By visualizing themselves succeeding in sales and repeating positive affirmations, salespeople can train their minds to focus on positive outcomes rather than negative ones.

- Learn from failure: Failure is a natural part of the sales process. Rather than letting failure discourage them, salespeople should use it as an opportunity to learn and improve. By analyzing what went wrong and identifying areas for improvement, salespeople can turn failure into a learning experience that helps them grow and succeed.

- Seek support: Sales can be a challenging and lonely profession. Salespeople should seek out support from colleagues, mentors, or coaches who can provide encouragement, feedback, and advice.

- Take action: Finally, the best way to overcome limiting beliefs and fear is to take action. Salespeople should focus on taking small, achievable steps towards their goals, rather than letting fear and self-doubt hold them back.

By adopting these strategies, salespeople can overcome limiting beliefs and fear, build confidence, and achieve greater success in sales.

❖ Building confidence and self esteem

Building confidence and self-esteem is crucial for success in sales. Here are some strategies that can help salespeople boost their confidence and self-esteem:

- Focus on strengths: Salespeople should focus on their strengths and the things they are good at. They should identify their unique selling points and use them to differentiate themselves from the competition.

- Celebrate successes: Celebrating successes, no matter how small, can help salespeople build confidence and self-esteem. Salespeople should acknowledge their achievements and use them as motivation to keep going.

- Set realistic goals: Setting realistic goals can help salespeople build confidence and self-esteem by providing a sense of accomplishment. Salespeople should set goals that are challenging but achievable, and break them down into smaller, manageable steps.

- Practice positive self-talk: Positive self-talk can help salespeople build confidence and self-esteem by replacing negative thoughts with positive ones. Salespeople should focus on their strengths, affirm their abilities, and remind themselves of past successes.

- Take care of physical health: Taking care of physical health can have a positive impact on mental health and self-esteem. Salespeople should eat a healthy diet, get enough sleep, exercise regularly, and practice relaxation techniques such as meditation or yoga.

- Learn new skills: Learning new skills can help salespeople build confidence and self-esteem by expanding their knowledge and abilities. Salespeople should seek out training opportunities, attend industry events, and read books and articles on sales and marketing.

- Seek feedback: Seeking feedback from colleagues, mentors, or coaches can help salespeople identify areas for improvement and build confidence and self-esteem. Salespeople should be open to constructive criticism and use it as an opportunity to learn and grow.

By adopting these strategies, salespeople can build confidence and self-esteem, which can help them succeed in sales and other areas of life.

Chapter 2; Sales Fundamentals

❖ Understanding your target market and ideal customers

Understanding your target market and ideal customers is crucial for success in sales. Here are some strategies that can help salespeople gain a deeper understanding of their target market and ideal customers:

- Conduct market research: Market research can help salespeople gather information about their target market, such as demographics, buying habits, and pain points. Salespeople can conduct surveys, interviews, and focus groups to gather this information.

- Create buyer personas: Buyer personas are fictional representations of your ideal customers based on market research and real customer data. Salespeople can create buyer personas to help them understand their customers' needs, preferences, and behaviors.

- Analyze customer data: Salespeople can analyze customer data such as sales history, customer feedback, and website analytics to gain insights into their customers' behaviors and preferences.

- Monitor social media: Social media platforms such as Twitter, Facebook, and LinkedIn can provide valuable insights into customer opinions and behaviors. Salespeople should monitor social media for mentions of their brand, competitors, and industry trends.

- Attend industry events: Attending industry events such as conferences and trade shows can provide salespeople with an opportunity to network with potential customers, learn about industry trends, and gather insights into their target market.

- Collaborate with marketing: Sales and marketing teams should collaborate to create a unified understanding of the target market and ideal customers. Marketing can provide sales with valuable insights and data to help them target their sales efforts effectively.

By adopting these strategies, salespeople can gain a deeper understanding of their target market and ideal customers, which can help them tailor their sales efforts to meet their customers' needs and preferences. This, in turn, can lead to increased sales and customer satisfaction.

❖ Building a strong value proposition

Building a strong value proposition is crucial for success in sales. A value proposition is a statement that describes the unique value that a product or service offers to customers. Here are some strategies that can help salespeople build a strong value proposition:

- Identify customer needs: Salespeople should identify their customers' needs and pain points. They should understand what their customers are looking for in a product or service and what problems they are trying to solve.

- Highlight unique features and benefits: Salespeople should highlight the unique features and benefits of their product or service. They should focus on what makes their product or service different from competitors and how it can help solve their customers' problems.

- Use clear and concise language: Salespeople should use clear and concise language to communicate their value proposition. They should avoid using jargon or technical terms that may be confusing to their customers.

- Emphasize value over price: Salespeople should emphasize the value of their product or service over its price. They should focus on how their product or service can save their customers time, money, or hassle, rather than just its cost.

- Address objections: Salespeople should anticipate and address any objections that customers may have about their product or service. They should be prepared to answer questions and provide evidence to support their claims.

- Test and refine: Salespeople should test their value proposition with customers and refine it based on feedback. They should be willing to make adjustments to their value proposition based on what resonates with their customers.

By adopting these strategies, salespeople can build a strong value proposition that resonates with their customers and sets them apart from competitors. A strong value proposition can help salespeople close more deals and build long-term relationships with customers.

❖ Identifying your unique selling proposition

Identifying your unique selling proposition (USP) is crucial for success in sales. A USP is a statement that describes what makes your product or service unique and why customers should choose it over competitors. Here are some strategies that can help you identify your USP:

- Conduct market research: Conduct market research to understand your competitors and your target market. Identify what your competitors are offering and what their strengths and weaknesses are. Also, gather insights into your customers' needs and preferences.

- Analyze your product or service: Analyze your product or service and identify what makes it unique. Look for features or benefits that your competitors don't offer, or that you do better than your competitors.

- Focus on customer needs: Focus on your customers' needs and how your product or service can solve their problems or address their pain points. Consider how your product or service can provide value and meet your customers' expectations in a way that competitors can't.

- Highlight benefits over features: Highlight the benefits of your product or service rather than just its features. Consider how your product or service can improve your customers' lives, save them time or money, or make their work easier.

- Test and refine: Test your USP with customers and refine it based on feedback. Consider how your USP resonates with your customers and whether it helps differentiate your product or service from competitors.

- Be specific: Be specific in your USP. Use language that is clear and concise, and avoid vague or generic statements. Focus on what makes your product or service truly unique and why customers should choose it over competitors.

By adopting these strategies, you can identify your unique selling proposition and use it to differentiate your product or service from competitors. A strong USP can help you stand out in a crowded market and attract more customers.

❖ Creating a compelling sales pitch

Creating a compelling sales pitch is essential for success in sales. Here are some strategies that can help you create a sales pitch that captures your customers' attention and persuades them to take action:

- Start with a strong opening: The opening of your sales pitch should be attention-grabbing and engaging. Use a story, a statistic, or a question to capture your customers' attention and draw them in.

- Focus on benefits, not features: Focus on the benefits of your product or service, rather than just its features. Explain how your product or service can improve your customers' lives, solve their problems, or meet their needs.

- Use clear and concise language: Use language that is clear and easy to understand. Avoid jargon or technical terms that may be confusing to your customers.

- Address objections: Anticipate and address any objections that your customers may have about your product or service. Be prepared to answer questions and provide evidence to support your claims.

- Create a sense of urgency: Create a sense of urgency by highlighting the consequences of not taking action or the benefits of acting now. Use language that suggests that time is running out, or that the opportunity is limited.

- Close with a clear call to action: Close your sales pitch with a clear call to action, such as "buy now," "sign up today," or "schedule a demo." Make it easy for your customers to take action and provide clear instructions on what they need to do next.

- Practice and refine: Practice your sales pitch and refine it based on feedback. Consider how your customers respond to your pitch and make adjustments as needed.

By adopting these strategies, you can create a compelling sales pitch that captures your customers' attention, addresses their concerns, and persuades them to take action. A strong sales pitch can help you close more deals and build long-term relationships with your customers.

Chapter 3; Sales Process

❖ Developing a sales process that works for you

Developing a sales process that works for you requires careful planning and experimentation. Here are some steps you can take to develop a sales process that suits your style and helps you achieve your goals:

- Define your sales goals: Identify your sales goals, such as the number of deals you want to close or the revenue you want to generate. Your sales process should be designed to help you achieve these goals.

- Map out your sales process: Map out the steps you need to take to move a prospect from initial contact to closing the sale. Identify the key touchpoints where you will engage with prospects and the actions you need to take at each stage of the process.

- Experiment with different approaches: Experiment with different approaches to find what works best for you. Try different sales tactics, such as cold calling, email marketing, or social media outreach, and track your results. Analyze what is working and what isn't, and adjust your approach accordingly.

- Use technology to automate and streamline your process: Use technology to automate and streamline your sales process. Tools like customer relationship management (CRM) software can help you track your interactions with prospects and automate routine tasks.

- Focus on building relationships: Focus on building relationships with your prospects and customers. Sales is a long-term game, and building trust and rapport with your customers is critical to your success.

- Continuously learn and improve: Continuously learn and improve your sales skills. Read books and articles on sales, attend sales training courses, and seek feedback from your peers and customers.

By following these steps, you can develop a sales process that works for you and helps you achieve your sales goals. Remember, the sales process is not set in stone and may need to be adjusted as your business evolves and your customers' needs change. Be flexible and willing to adapt your approach as needed.

❖ Understanding the stages of the sales process

Understanding the stages of the sales process is essential for effective sales. Here are the typical stages of the sales process:

- Prospecting: The first stage of the sales process is prospecting, where you identify potential customers who may be interested in your product or service. This may involve researching companies, attending networking events, or using marketing tactics to generate leads.

- Qualifying: In the qualifying stage, you determine whether a prospect is a good fit for your product or service. This involves assessing their needs, budget, decision-making process, and timeline.

- Needs assessment: In this stage, you ask questions to uncover the prospect's needs and challenges. This helps you understand how your product or service can address their pain points and provide value.

- Presenting: The presenting stage involves showcasing your product or service and how it meets the prospect's needs. This may involve a demonstration, a proposal, or a product sample.

- Handling objections: In the objections stage, you address any concerns or objections the prospect may have about your product or service. This may involve providing more information, offering testimonials or case studies, or addressing any misconceptions.

- Closing: The closing stage involves asking for the sale and finalizing the details of the transaction. This may involve negotiating price or terms, providing a contract or invoice, and securing payment.

- Follow-up: The final stage of the sales process is follow-up, where you maintain contact with the customer after the sale. This may involve checking in to ensure customer satisfaction, upselling or cross-selling, or requesting referrals or testimonials.

By understanding these stages and tailoring your approach to each stage, you can increase your chances of success in sales. Remember, the sales process is not linear, and prospects may move back and forth between stages. Be flexible and adjust your approach as needed to meet the prospect's needs and move them towards a sale.

❖ Qualifying leads and prospects

Qualifying leads and prospects is a critical step in the sales process. By qualifying your leads and prospects, you can focus your efforts on those who are most likely to become customers and avoid wasting time on those who are not a good fit. Here are some steps you can take to qualify leads and prospects:

- Identify your ideal customer: Start by identifying your ideal customer, including factors such as company size, industry, location, and budget.

- Research potential prospects: Use a variety of resources to research potential prospects, including social media, business directories, and trade publications. Look for prospects who match your ideal customer profile.

- Ask qualifying questions: When you first make contact with a potential prospect, ask qualifying questions to determine if they are a good fit for your product or service. These may include questions about their needs, budget, decision-making process, and timeline.

- Use a lead scoring system: Use a lead scoring system to rank your prospects based on their likelihood of becoming customers. This may involve assigning points for factors such as company size, budget, and decision-maker status.

- Use a customer relationship management (CRM) system: Use a CRM system to track your interactions with prospects and monitor their progress through the sales process.

- Be willing to disqualify leads: Be willing to disqualify leads who are not a good fit for your product or service. This may involve politely declining to pursue the opportunity or referring the prospect to a competitor who may be better suited to meet their needs.

By taking these steps, you can qualify leads and prospects effectively and focus your efforts on those who are most likely to become customers. Remember, the goal is not to close as many deals as possible, but to close the right deals that will benefit both your business and your customers.

❖ Building rapport and trust with customers

Building rapport and trust with customers is essential for successful sales. When customers trust and feel comfortable with you, they are more likely to buy from you and to become loyal customers. Here are some tips for building rapport and trust with customers:

- Listen actively: Listen carefully to your customers' needs and concerns, and show that you understand and empathize with them.

- Be honest and transparent: Be upfront and honest about what you can and cannot do for your customers. Don't make promises you can't keep, and be transparent about pricing, timelines, and any potential risks.

- Demonstrate expertise: Demonstrate your expertise and knowledge of your product or service. This will help build credibility and trust with your customers.

- Show interest in the customer: Show genuine interest in your customers as individuals. Ask about their business, their goals, and their challenges, and find ways to help them achieve success.

- Communicate clearly: Communicate clearly and effectively with your customers, both in person and in writing. Avoid using technical jargon or language that may be confusing.

- Follow up: Follow up with your customers after the sale to ensure their satisfaction and to address any issues that may arise.

- Personalize your approach: Tailor your approach to each individual customer. Show that you understand their unique needs and preferences, and find ways to personalize your product or service to meet those needs.

By following these tips, you can build rapport and trust with your customers and increase your chances of successful sales. Remember, building relationships takes time and effort, but the benefits can be significant for both you and your customers.

Chapter 4; communication skills

❖ Developing effective communication skills

Developing effective communication skills is critical for success in sales. Here are some tips to help you improve your communication skills:

- Listen actively: Active listening involves paying attention to what the other person is saying, clarifying any misunderstandings, and responding appropriately. This helps build rapport and trust with your customers.

- Use clear and concise language: Use clear and concise language to communicate your ideas effectively. Avoid using technical jargon or language that may be confusing.

- Speak confidently: Speak confidently and clearly, using a strong and engaging voice. This helps convey authority and professionalism.

- Use body language: Use positive body language, such as maintaining eye contact, smiling, and using open gestures. This helps convey interest and engagement.

- Practice empathy: Put yourself in your customer's shoes and try to see things from their perspective. This helps you understand their needs and concerns and communicate more effectively.

- Tailor your communication style: Tailor your communication style to the individual customer. Some customers may prefer a more formal approach, while others may prefer a more casual and friendly tone.

- Use visual aids: Use visual aids, such as graphs or diagrams, to help explain complex ideas or data more effectively.

- Practice active feedback: Practice active feedback by seeking feedback from others on your communication style and adjusting as needed.

By practicing these communication skills, you can become a more effective communicator and increase your chances of success in sales. Remember, effective communication is a two-way street, so be sure to actively listen and respond to your customers' needs and concerns.

❖ Listening actively

Active listening is an important skill for anyone in sales or any other profession that requires effective communication. Here are some tips for listening actively:

- Pay attention: Focus on the speaker and give them your undivided attention. Avoid distractions, such as checking your phone or thinking about other things.

- Clarify: Clarify any misunderstandings by asking questions or repeating back what the speaker said. This helps ensure that you understand their message accurately.

- Show empathy: Show empathy and understanding by acknowledging the speaker's emotions and feelings. This helps build rapport and trust with the speaker.

- Avoid interrupting: Avoid interrupting the speaker, even if you disagree or have something to add. Wait until they have finished speaking before responding.

- Reflect: Reflect on what the speaker said and think about how it relates to the conversation or the sales process. This helps you process the information and respond effectively.

- Summarize: Summarize the speaker's message to ensure that you have understood it correctly. This helps prevent misunderstandings and ensures that you are on the same page.

By practicing active listening, you can become a more effective communicator and build stronger relationships with your customers. Remember, communication is a two-way street, and active listening is just as important as speaking clearly and effectively.

❖ Asking powerful question

Asking powerful questions is a key skill in sales that can help you understand your customers' needs, build rapport and trust, and guide the conversation towards a successful outcome. Here are some tips for asking powerful questions:

- Be open-ended: Ask open-ended questions that encourage the customer to share their thoughts and feelings. These questions cannot be answered with a simple "yes" or "no" and can help you gather more information.

- Ask for specifics: Ask specific questions that help you understand the customer's needs, goals, and challenges. This helps you tailor your pitch to their unique situation.

- Use "why" and "how" questions: "Why" and "how" questions can help you dig deeper into the customer's motivations and thought processes. For example, "Why is this important to you?" or "How do you see this working in your business?"

- Avoid leading questions: Avoid leading questions that suggest a particular answer or steer the conversation in a particular direction. This can be seen as manipulative and may damage the rapport and trust you have built with the customer.

- Be curious: Show genuine curiosity and interest in the customer's situation. This helps build rapport and trust and encourages the customer to share more information.

- Listen actively: Listen actively to the customer's responses and use their answers to guide the conversation towards a successful outcome.

By asking powerful questions, you can gain valuable insights into your customer's needs and challenges, build rapport and trust, and guide the conversation towards a successful outcome. Remember to be genuine, curious, and open-minded in your approach, and use the customer's answers to guide your next steps.

❖ Overcoming objections and handling rejection

In sales, objections and rejections are inevitable. Here are some tips for overcoming objections and handling rejections effectively:

- Understand the objection: Listen carefully to the objection and try to understand the customer's concern. Ask follow-up questions to clarify their objection and gather more information.

- Address the objection: Address the customer's objection directly and offer a solution or alternative that addresses their concern. Be confident in your response and use specific examples or case studies to support your argument.

- Handle rejection gracefully: Rejections are a part of the sales process, and it's important to handle them gracefully. Thank the customer for their time and consideration and offer to follow up at a later date.

- Stay positive: It's important to stay positive and maintain a can-do attitude, even in the face of rejection. Use rejection as an opportunity to learn and improve your approach.

- Follow up: Don't give up on a potential sale after the first objection or rejection. Follow up with the customer at a later date and offer additional information or resources that may address their concerns.

- Build relationships: Building strong relationships with customers is key to overcoming objections and handling rejections. Focus on building rapport and trust with your customers and demonstrating your value as a partner.

Remember, objections and rejections are not personal, and they are an opportunity to learn and improve your approach. By addressing objections directly, staying positive, and building strong relationships with your customers, you can overcome objections and turn rejections into opportunities for growth.

Chapter 5; The sales technique

❖ Understanding different sales technique

There are several sales techniques that salespeople can use to improve their effectiveness and close more deals. Here are some of the most common sales techniques:

- Consultative selling: This approach focuses on building a relationship with the customer and understanding their needs and challenges before offering a solution. It involves asking questions, listening actively, and tailoring the pitch to the customer's unique situation.

- Solution selling: This approach focuses on presenting a solution to the customer's problem, rather than simply selling a product. It involves asking questions to identify the customer's needs, offering a customized solution, and highlighting the benefits of the solution.

- Challenger selling: This approach challenges the customer's assumptions and offers a new perspective on their challenges. It involves being assertive and taking a consultative approach to identify areas where the customer can improve their business.

- Relationship selling: This approach focuses on building a long-term relationship with the customer. It involves being responsive, reliable, and trustworthy and providing ongoing support and value beyond the initial sale.

- Social selling: This approach uses social media to build relationships and engage with potential customers. It involves using social media platforms to share content, engage with prospects, and build trust and credibility.

- Direct selling: This approach involves selling directly to the customer, often through in-person or online presentations. It involves building rapport and trust with the customer, understanding their needs, and presenting the benefits of the product or service.

Ultimately, the most effective sales technique will depend on the salesperson's strengths, the customer's needs, and the industry and market in which they operate. By understanding the different sales techniques available, salespeople can tailor their approach to meet the needs of their customers and improve their effectiveness.

❖ Upselling and cross-selling

Upselling and cross-selling are two common sales techniques used to increase the value of a sale and improve customer satisfaction.

Upselling involves encouraging a customer to purchase a more expensive or premium version of a product or service they are considering. For example, a salesperson might suggest that a customer upgrade to a more powerful version of a software product or a more luxurious version of a hotel room.

Cross-selling involves recommending complementary products or services that the customer may be interested in. For example, a salesperson selling a laptop might recommend a laptop case, a mouse, or other accessories.

Both upselling and cross-selling can be effective ways to increase revenue and improve customer satisfaction. However, it's important to use these techniques ethically and focus on providing value to the customer rather than simply increasing the size of the sale.

Here are some tips for effective upselling and cross-selling:

- Understand the customer's needs: Before suggesting an upsell or cross-sell, make sure you understand the customer's needs and preferences.

- Suggest relevant products or services: Only suggest products or services that are relevant to the customer's needs or the product they are already considering.

- Highlight the benefits: Explain the benefits of the upsell or cross-sell and how it can help the customer achieve their goals or solve their problems.

- Be transparent: Be transparent about the price and any additional costs associated with the upsell or cross-sell.

- Don't push too hard: Avoid pushing the customer too hard or making them feel pressured to make a purchase. Be respectful of their decision, and focus on providing value and building trust.

- Follow up: After the sale, follow up with the customer to ensure they are satisfied with their purchase and address any concerns they may have.

By using upselling and cross-selling effectively, salespeople can increase the value of a sale, improve customer satisfaction, and build long-term relationships with their customers.

❖ Closing the sales

Closing the sale is the final stage of the sales process where the salesperson attempts to persuade the customer to make a purchase. Here are some tips for closing the sale:

- Ask for the sale: One of the simplest and most effective ways to close a sale is to simply ask for it. Ask the customer if they are ready to make a purchase or if they have any questions or concerns that need to be addressed before making a decision.

- Recap the benefits: Recap the benefits of the product or service and how it can help the customer solve their problems or achieve their goals. Remind them of the value they will receive from the purchase.

- Address objections: If the customer has any objections or concerns, address them directly and provide evidence or examples to alleviate their concerns.

- Offer incentives: Offer incentives to encourage the customer to make a purchase, such as a discount, a free trial, or a bonus product.

- Create a sense of urgency: Create a sense of urgency by emphasizing the need to act quickly or highlighting any time-limited offers or promotions.

- Provide reassurance: Provide reassurance to the customer by offering a guarantee, warranty, or after-sales support.

- Follow up: After the sale, follow up with the customer to ensure they are satisfied with their purchase and address any concerns they may have.

It's important to remember that closing the sale is not about pressuring the customer or tricking them into making a purchase. It's about providing value, building trust, and helping the customer make an informed decision that meets their needs and goals. By following these tips and focusing on the customer's needs and preferences, salespeople can improve their closing rate and build long-term relationships with their customers.

❖ Follow-up and customer retention

Follow-up and customer retention are critical components of the sales process that help salespeople build long-term relationships with their customers and generate repeat business. Here are some tips for effective follow-up and customer retention:

- Follow up promptly: After making a sale, follow up with the customer promptly to ensure they are satisfied with their purchase and address any concerns they may have.

- Provide after-sales support: Provide after-sales support to ensure the customer is able to use the product or service effectively and get the most value out of their purchase.

- Personalize communication: Personalize your communication with the customer and make them feel valued and appreciated. Use their name and reference previous conversations to show that you remember them.

- Offer additional value: Offer additional value to the customer by providing helpful tips, advice, or resources related to their purchase. This can help build trust and loyalty.

- Address concerns promptly: If the customer has any concerns or issues, address them promptly and provide solutions or alternatives to alleviate their concerns.

- Stay in touch: Stay in touch with the customer and maintain regular communication through email, phone, or social media. This can help keep you top-of-mind and build long-term relationships.

- Provide incentives: Provide incentives to encourage repeat business, such as loyalty rewards, special offers, or exclusive content.

By focusing on follow-up and customer retention, salespeople can build long-term relationships with their customers, generate repeat business, and increase customer satisfaction and loyalty.

Chapter 6; Sales tools and technology
- ❖ Using sales tools and technology to improve efficiency

Sales tools and technology can help salespeople improve their efficiency and productivity by automating repetitive tasks, streamlining workflows, and providing valuable insights and analytics. Here are some examples of sales tools and technologies that can be used to improve efficiency:

- Customer Relationship Management (CRM) software: CRM software allows salespeople to manage their customer interactions and sales pipeline in a centralized platform. It can automate tasks such as lead capture, follow-up, and reporting, and provide insights into customer behavior and preferences.

- Sales automation tools: Sales automation tools such as email automation, social media scheduling, and task management software can help salespeople save time and streamline their workflows.

- Sales intelligence tools: Sales intelligence tools such as lead scoring, prospecting, and competitive intelligence software can help salespeople identify and prioritize their best leads and opportunities.

- Video conferencing software: Video conferencing software such as Zoom or Google Meet can help salespeople conduct virtual sales calls and meetings with customers, reducing the need for in-person meetings and travel.

- Mobile apps: Mobile apps such as sales tracking, note-taking, and productivity software can help salespeople stay organized and productive while on-the-go.

By leveraging these sales tools and technologies, salespeople can streamline their workflows, save time, and focus on building relationships with their customers, ultimately leading to increased efficiency and productivity.

❖ CRM system and sales automation

CRM (Customer Relationship Management) systems are software platforms designed to manage and track customer interactions, sales leads, and marketing campaigns. They provide a central database for storing customer information, allowing sales teams to access the information they need to effectively manage customer relationships and close deals.

CRM systems can also include sales automation features, such as automated email campaigns, task automation, and lead scoring, to help streamline the sales process and improve efficiency. Here are some ways that CRM systems and sales automation can benefit sales teams:

- Improved lead management: CRM systems can help sales teams manage and prioritize leads by tracking lead sources, lead interactions, and lead scores, enabling sales reps to focus on the most promising opportunities.

- Streamlined sales process: CRM systems can automate tasks such as lead nurturing, scheduling follow-ups, and sending reminders, allowing sales reps to focus on high-value activities, such as building relationships with prospects and closing deals.

- Increased efficiency: Sales automation features in CRM systems can help reduce manual data entry, eliminate repetitive tasks, and improve the accuracy and consistency of sales data, leading to increased efficiency and productivity.

- Enhanced customer insights: CRM systems can provide valuable insights into customer behavior, preferences, and buying patterns, allowing sales teams to tailor their approach and messaging to individual customers and improve customer satisfaction.

- Improved collaboration: CRM systems can provide a centralized platform for sales teams to collaborate and share information, allowing for better communication, more effective teamwork, and increased sales success.

Overall, CRM systems and sales automation can help sales teams streamline their workflows, improve efficiency, and build stronger relationships with customers, ultimately leading to increased sales and revenue.

❖ Social media and digital marketing

Social media and digital marketing are essential components of a successful sales strategy in today's digital age. Here are some ways that social media and digital marketing can benefit sales teams:

- Increased visibility and reach: Social media platforms such as Facebook, Instagram, Twitter, and LinkedIn provide a vast audience for businesses to reach potential customers, allowing sales teams to connect with a broader audience and increase brand visibility.

- Targeted advertising: Social media and digital marketing allow businesses to target specific audiences with tailored messaging and advertising campaigns, enabling sales teams to reach potential customers based on demographics, interests, and behaviors.
- Cost-effective: Social media and digital marketing can be more cost-effective than traditional advertising methods, allowing businesses to reach a larger audience while staying within their budget.

- Enhanced customer engagement: Social media and digital marketing can help businesses engage with customers in real-time, responding to comments, questions, and concerns, and providing valuable insights into customer behavior and preferences.

- Valuable insights and analytics: Social media and digital marketing provide valuable data and insights into customer behavior, preferences, and interests, allowing sales teams to refine their approach and messaging based on data-driven insights.

By leveraging social media and digital marketing, sales teams can reach a broader audience, target potential customers more effectively, engage with customers in real-time, and gather valuable insights and analytics, ultimately leading to increased sales and revenue.

❖ Networking and building relationships

Networking and building relationships are crucial skills for sales professionals. Building strong relationships with customers and prospects is essential to establishing trust and credibility, which can lead to increased sales and customer loyalty. Here are some ways to effectively network and build relationships:

- Attend networking events: Attend networking events in your industry to meet potential customers and business partners. Be sure to bring business cards and have a clear pitch ready to explain your product or service.

- Leverage social media: Use social media platforms like LinkedIn to connect with prospects and build relationships with industry leaders. Share valuable content, engage with your connections, and build relationships over time.

- Follow up and stay in touch: After meeting someone, follow up with them within a day or two to thank them for their time and express your interest in working with them. Stay in touch with regular check-ins, share helpful resources or insights, and be available to answer questions.

- Provide value: Focus on providing value to your prospects and customers. This can mean sharing industry insights or resources, connecting them with other professionals in your network, or offering a personalized solution to their specific needs.

- Be authentic: Be genuine and authentic in your interactions. Build trust by listening to your customers' needs, providing honest feedback, and showing a willingness to learn from them.

Overall, networking and building relationships require patience, persistence, and a genuine interest in helping others. By building strong relationships with your customers and prospects, you can establish yourself as a trusted partner and increase your chances of success in sales.

Chapter 7; Sales Leadership

❖ Developing sales leadership skills

Developing sales leadership skills is essential for sales professionals who aspire to take on leadership roles within their organizations. Here are some key skills and strategies to help you develop your sales leadership skills:

- Develop a growth mindset: As a sales leader, you must have a growth mindset and be willing to learn from your experiences and mistakes. Embrace challenges as opportunities to learn and grow, and encourage your team to do the same.

- Build a high-performing team: As a sales leader, your job is to build and lead a high-performing sales team. This requires recruiting top talent, providing ongoing training and development, setting clear expectations, and holding your team accountable for results.

- Lead by example: As a sales leader, you must lead by example and set the tone for your team. Demonstrate the behaviors and values you expect from your team, such as integrity, hard work, and a customer-centric approach.

- Communicate effectively: Communication is a critical skill for sales leaders. You must be able to communicate your vision, goals, and expectations clearly to your team, as well as provide feedback, coaching, and recognition when needed.

- Analyze and optimize sales processes: As a sales leader, you must have a deep understanding of your sales processes and be able to analyze data to identify areas for improvement. Use data to optimize your sales processes, track key metrics, and make data-driven decisions.

- Build strong relationships: Sales leaders must build strong relationships with customers, prospects, and other stakeholders. Focus on building trust, providing value, and developing long-term partnerships.

- Embrace innovation: Sales leaders must be open to new ideas and innovations that can help their teams succeed. Stay up-to-date on the latest technologies, trends, and best practices in sales, and be willing to experiment and take risks.

By developing these sales leadership skills, you can become an effective leader and drive success for your team and your organization.

❖ Managing a sales team

Managing a sales team can be a challenging task, but with the right approach and strategies, you can help your team reach their full potential and achieve their sales goals. Here are some key tips for managing a sales team:

- Set clear goals and expectations: Provide your team with clear goals and expectations, and communicate them effectively. Make sure they understand what they are working towards and what success looks like.

- Provide ongoing training and development: Ensure your team has the necessary training and development to be successful in their roles. Offer coaching, mentoring, and opportunities for professional development.

- Hold your team accountable: Set up a system for tracking and measuring performance and hold your team accountable for their results. Provide regular feedback and coaching to help them improve and reach their goals.

- Foster a positive and collaborative team culture: Create a positive and collaborative team culture where everyone feels supported and valued. Encourage team members to share their successes and challenges, and celebrate wins together.

- Use data to make informed decisions: Analyze sales data to identify trends, opportunities, and areas for improvement. Use this data to make informed decisions about sales strategy, process optimization, and resource allocation.

- Motivate and inspire your team: Sales can be a high-pressure and stressful job, so it's important to motivate and inspire your team to stay focused and engaged. Recognize and reward good performance, and create a positive and supportive work environment.

- Be a strong communicator: As a sales team manager, you must be a strong communicator. Be available to your team for questions, concerns, and feedback, and communicate important updates and changes effectively.

By implementing these strategies, you can help your sales team succeed and achieve their goals, ultimately driving success for your organization.

❖ Motivating and inspiring your team

Motivating and inspiring your sales team is critical to their success and the success of your organization. Here are some strategies you can use to motivate and inspire your team:

- Lead by example: Be a role model for your team. Demonstrate a strong work ethic, positive attitude, and commitment to success. Show your team that you are invested in their success and that you are willing to do what it takes to help them achieve their goals.

- Set challenging but achievable goals: Set goals that are challenging but achievable. This will help your team stay motivated and focused on achieving their objectives. Celebrate their successes along the way and provide positive feedback and recognition.

- Provide regular feedback: Provide regular feedback to your team members on their performance. This will help them understand where they need to improve and where they are excelling. Use positive reinforcement to build confidence and inspire your team.

- Offer incentives and rewards: Offer incentives and rewards for achieving sales goals. This can be anything from cash bonuses to recognition and praise. Make sure that the rewards are meaningful and tailored to the individual's interests and needs.

- Foster a positive work environment: Create a positive and supportive work environment where your team feels valued and supported. Encourage teamwork, collaboration, and open communication. Show your team that you care about them as people, not just as employees.

- Provide ongoing training and development: Offer ongoing training and development opportunities to your team. This will help them stay up-to-date with the latest sales techniques and technologies, and will help them improve their skills and knowledge.

- Encourage creativity and innovation: Encourage your team to think creatively and come up with new ideas for sales strategies and approaches. This will help them feel empowered and engaged in their work, and will help your organization stay competitive.

By implementing these strategies, you can help motivate and inspire your sales team to achieve their goals and drive success for your organization.

❖ Creating a culture of success

Creating a culture of success is crucial for building a high-performing sales team. Here are some key strategies for creating a culture of success:

- Set a clear vision and goals: Define a clear vision and set achievable goals that are aligned with your organization's mission. Communicate this vision and goals to your team, and make sure they understand how their work contributes to the overall success of the organization.

- Encourage teamwork and collaboration: Foster a culture of teamwork and collaboration by encouraging your team to work together and share ideas. Provide opportunities for team-building activities, and recognize and reward team successes.

- Celebrate successes and learn from failures: Celebrate successes and learn from failures. Use successes as opportunities to reinforce the behaviors and strategies that led to success, and use failures as opportunities to learn and improve.

- Provide ongoing training and development: Offer ongoing training and development opportunities to your team to help them stay up-to-date with the latest sales techniques and technologies. Encourage your team to share their knowledge and expertise with each other.

- Foster a positive work environment: Create a positive and supportive work environment where your team feels valued and supported. Encourage open communication, and be available to your team to address any concerns or issues they may have.

- Set high standards and hold everyone accountable: Set high standards for performance, and hold everyone accountable for meeting those standards. Provide regular feedback and coaching to help your team members improve.

- Recognize and reward success: Recognize and reward success to reinforce positive behaviors and motivate your team. Offer incentives and rewards for achieving sales goals, and make sure they are meaningful and tailored to the individual's interests and needs.

By implementing these strategies, you can create a culture of success that will help your sales team achieve their goals and drive success for your organization.

Conclusion:

Sales mastery is an ongoing journey that requires dedication, hard work and a commitment to continuous learning and improvement. By mastering the essential elements of sales, you can increase your revenue, build strong customer relationships and achieve your business goals. Use the strategies and tips outlined in this book to develop your own sales mastery and achieve success in your sales career or business.